C000214697

Liberty Phi

CAPRICORN

INTRODUCTION

Astrology is all about the planets in our skies and what energy and characteristics influence us. From ancient times, people have wanted to understand the rhythms of life and looked to the skies and their celestial bodies for inspiration, and the ancient constellations are there in the 12 zodiac signs we recognise from astrology. The Ancient Greeks devised narratives related to myths and legends about their celestial ancestors, to which they referred to make decisions and choices. Roman mythology did the same and over the years these ancient wisdoms became refined into today's modern astrology.

The configuration of the planets in the sky at the time and place of our birth is unique to each and every one of us, and what this means and how it plays out throughout our lives is both fascinating and informative. Just knowing which planet rules your sun sign is the beginning of an exploratory journey that can provide you with a useful tool for life.

Understanding the meaning, energetic nature and power of each planet, where this sits in your birth chart and what this might mean is all important information and linked to your date, place and time of birth, relevant *only* to you. Completely individual, the way in which you can work with the power of the planets comes from understanding their qualities and how this might influence the position in which they sit in your chart.

What knowledge of astrology can give you is the tools for working out how a planetary pattern might influence you, because of its relationship to your particular planetary configuration and circumstances. Each sun sign has a set of characteristics linked to its ruling planet – for example, Capricorn is ruled by Saturn – and, in turn, to each of the 12 Houses (see page 81) that form the structure of every individual's birth chart (see page 78). Once you know the meanings of these and how these relate to different areas of your life, you can begin to work out what might be relevant to you when, for example, you read in a magazine horoscope that there's a Full Moon in Capricorn or that Jupiter is transiting Mars.

Each of the 12 astrological or zodiac sun signs is ruled by a planet (see page 52) and looking at a planet's characteristics will give you an indication of the influences brought to bear on each sign. It's useful to have a general understanding of these influences, because your birth chart includes many of them, in different house or planetary configurations, which gives you information about how uniquely *you* you are. Also included in this book are the minor planets (see page 102), also relevant to the information your chart provides.

CAPRICORN

Our sun sign is determined by the date of our birth wherever we are born, and if you are a Capricorn you were born between December 22nd and January 19th. Bear in mind, however, that if you were born on one or other of those actual dates it's worth checking your *time* of birth, if you know it, against the year you were born and where. That's because no one is born 'on the cusp' (see page 78) and because there will be a moment on those days when Sagittarius shifts to Capricorn, and Capricorn shifts to Aquarius. It's well worth a check, especially if you've never felt quite convinced that the characteristics of your designated sun sign match your own.

The constellation of Capricorn is a medium-sized one that takes a triangular shape depicting a sea goat, with Delta Capricorni the brightest star in the constellation, situated in the tail. In Greek myth, the sea goat symbolises Pan, traditionally half-man half-faun, who escaped a monster by acquiring a fishtail and swimming away from danger, and in this form is depicted among the sky's constellations.

Capricorn is ruled by Saturn, sometimes called the taskmaster of the skies because this planet is all about reaping the reward of effort rather than luck. The Roman god Saturn sowed the seed and patiently tended its growth until harvest.

An earth sign (like Taurus and Virgo), Capricorn benefits from being grounded in attitude, taking a relatively pragmatic approach to life, and they are also good at not being knocked off course by distractions. This is also a cardinal sign (like Libra, Aries and Cancer), so Capricorns are about initiating action too, which means they don't get stuck. There's a good, generally optimistic, energy about what's required to get things done and they don't shirk the work necessary to achieve this; in fact, they often relish it.

This combination of being able to enjoy the process of work in order to achieve is an enviable trait because it means Capricorn often succeeds long after others give up, and while bright ideas are easy to initiate, being able to deliver on these is a real gift.

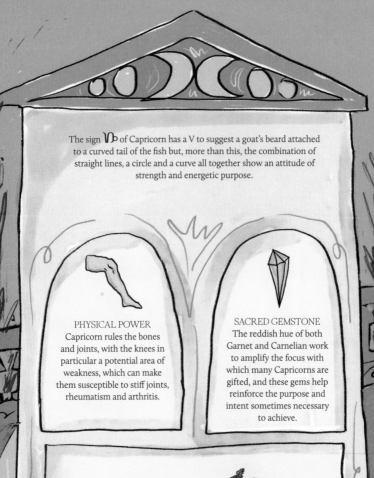

The sign ♑ of Capricorn has a V to suggest a goat's beard attached to a curved tail of the fish but, more than this, the combination of straight lines, a circle and a curve all together show an attitude of strength and energetic purpose.

PHYSICAL POWER
Capricorn rules the bones and joints, with the knees in particular a potential area of weakness, which can make them susceptible to stiff joints, rheumatism and arthritis.

SACRED GEMSTONE
The reddish hue of both Garnet and Carnelian work to amplify the focus with which many Capricorns are gifted, and these gems help reinforce the purpose and intent sometimes necessary to achieve.

OPPOSITE SIGN
Cancer

The other symbol for Capricorn is that of the mountain goat, sure-footedly making its ascent, which is very much how this sun sign progresses through life. There's a sense of commitment to the climb necessary in order to achieve the recognition, praise or accolades that can come from their efforts, on which their reputation can rest. This can be an important motivator for many Capricorns who deliberately seek to secure a public profile in some form, whether in person or through their work. For this trait, Capricorn is often described as ambitious for success in both life and public recognition, which they often achieve, but this tends to occur as a by-product of the success they achieve through their work.

Capricorns are often very conscious of the limitations of time and tend not to waste it: is one life going to be long enough to achieve everything they set out to do? This is Saturn's influence, the planet associated with time and limitations, so Capricorn often feels as if they are running against the clock, hence their focus-fuelled motivation. They will often opt to complete something today rather than leave it until tomorrow, even if it means putting in the extra hours. Plus, thanks to that streak of initiative, Capricorn assembles the known facts faster than most and acts on them without vacillation, all of which *saves* time – time to go out and have some fun!

Capricorn is not a sign that wastes time obsessing or ruminating on alternatives as they find making decisions easy, basing them on what they do know and not concerning themselves with what they don't. It would be easy to think that all this due diligence isn't very creative but that too would be a mistake. Capricorns are by nature extremely creative, particularly with the tools of their mind, and because they tend not to be the worriers of the zodiac, their creativity isn't hampered by unnecessary negative or restrictive thoughts.

Saturn can instil a touch of austerity, which gives Capricorn a reputation for being serious-minded and not much fun. While many Capricorns may have to learn to lighten up a little, or be reminded that all work and no play can make them dull company, many have a dry and responsive sense of humour, capable of witty repartee, and often turn out to be the unexpected life and soul of the party.

Unlike some of their astrological counterparts, it's not always easy to guess a Capricorn because their *joie de vivre* and energy can be hidden behind a serious-looking and rather observant mask, making them at times seem rather reserved. This trait can sometimes be misunderstood as not caring, and occasionally get in the way of a range of relationships. But once Capricorn feels on a stable footing they relax and prove to be the most consistent, insightful and fun friends. It's not that they're insecure as such, it's just that they need to know where they stand in relation to others, and once that's established, Capricorn makes the best partner or friend.

THE MOON IN YOUR CHART

While your zodiac sign is your sun sign, making you a sun sign Capricorn, the Moon also plays a role in your birth chart and if you know the time and place of your birth, along with your birth date, you can get your birth chart done (see page 78). From this you can discover in which zodiac sign your Moon is positioned in your chart.

The Moon reflects the characteristics of who you are at the time of your birth, your innate personality, how you express yourself and how you are seen by others. This is in contrast to our sun sign which indicates the more dominant characteristics we reveal as we travel through life. The Moon also represents the feminine in our natal chart (the Sun the masculine) and the sign in which our Moon falls can indicate how we express the feminine side of our personality. Looking at the two signs together in our charts immediately creates a balance.

MOON IN CAPRICORN

The Moon spends roughly 2.5 days in each zodiac sign as it moves through all 12 signs during its monthly cycle. This means that the Moon is regularly in Capricorn, and it can be useful to know when this occurs and in particular when we have a New Moon or a Full Moon in Capricorn because these are good times for you to focus your energy and intentions.

A New Moon is always the start of a new cycle, an opportunity to set new intentions for the coming month, and when this is in your own sign, Capricorn, you can benefit from this additional energy and support. The Full Moon is an opportunity to reflect on the culmination of your earlier intentions.

NEW MOON
IN CAPRICORN AFFIRMATION

'I will use the energy of the earth to achieve
what I have to do, taking each step, one after
another, in good faith, to work towards the
progress I wish to make.'

FULL MOON
IN CAPRICORN AFFIRMATION

'The Full Moon's light shows me that my endeavour
is its own reward, and from this I will trust that my
higher purpose will be revealed to me.'

CAPRICORN HEALTH

Capricorn rules the bones and the joints in general and the knees in particular. Given this sign is generally strong in body and mind, any problems in youth may be from accidents or sporting injuries where the knees can be vulnerable. Later in life, problems with rheumatoid or osteo-arthritis may emerge, but by keeping in general good health through diet and exercise the impact of these can often be lessened.

Keeping healthy and strong throughout life can often be an ambition for Capricorn, and they are more likely than some signs to have a gym membership and actually *use* it regularly. Saturn helps here too, because the emphasis is always on reaping what you sow: if you keep fit you will feel better and those joints will last longer. Capricorn isn't particularly competitive with others, so playing team sports or trying to beat someone in a tennis match is only really of interest because of its physical enjoyment. Running, as long as care is taken of the knees, may be of more interest, particularly as Capricorn is likely to have the stamina for long distance. As an action sign, running will appeal, while gentler activities like yoga may be of less interest.

POWER UP
YOUR
CAPRICORN
ENERGY

There are often moments or periods when we feel uninspired, demotivated and low in energy. At these times it's worth working with your innate sun sign energy to power up again, and paying attention to what Capricorn relishes and needs can help support both physical and mental health.

Capricorns have a natural instinct for what works for them when it comes to revitalising their earthy spirit and they also know the value of looking up and out, rather than at their feet, as they put one foot in front of the other to improve their mood. The combination of exercise, daylight and a change of scenery combine to help Capricorn power up again, particularly after a period of hard work for which they are renowned. And often, if they have something to think through, a problem or a strategy that needs their concentration, Capricorns find that taking a walk alone works well, rather than ruminating on it or discussing it with others.

For inspiration, however, solitary activities may work less well. Then socialising will definitely help, particularly if there's a cultural aspect to it like visiting an art gallery or museum, the theatre, music concert or cinema, all of which can really help to lift personal creativity and the spirits. While Capricorn isn't a brooder, and isn't particularly prone to anxiety, they can sometimes forget the value of seeking out stimulating new ideas by means of exposing themselves to the beauty of life around them, whether this is natural landscapes or works of art.

Capricorn needs to remember the power of good nutrients too. They usually eat well, if simply, but can benefit from foods that help restimulate their appetite and energy, as well as greater variety. Adequate calcium will help their bones, and this can be found in dairy products but also in green vegetables, almond and Brazil nuts, sardines, tofu, tinned kidney or butter beans and dried apricots and figs. What is also needed for calcium absorption is vitamin D, much of which we gain from 20–30 minutes exposure to ultraviolet light daily.

Capricorns can also pep up their foods using herbs and spices, which also help stimulate the appetite if it's feeling a little jaded. Avoid adding salt but pique flavours with oregano, rosemary or sage, while turmeric, ginger and garlic will add flavour and also help manage any inflammation in the joints.

Utilise a New Moon in Capricorn with a ritual to set your intentions and power up: light a candle, use essential oil of neroli to lift your mood and energise (this oil blends well with rose and bergamot), focus your thoughts on the change you wish to see and allow time to meditate on this. Place your gemstone (see page 13) in the moonlight. Write down your intentions and keep in a safe place. Meditate on the New Moon in Capricorn affirmation (see page 21).

At a Full Moon in Capricorn you will have the benefit of the Sun's reflected light to help illuminate what is working for you and what you can let go, because the Full Moon brings clarity. Take the time to meditate on the Full Moon in Capricorn affirmation (see page 21). Light a candle, place your gemstone in the moonlight and make a note of your thoughts and feelings, strengthened by the Moon in your sign.

CAPRICORN'S SPIRITUAL HOME

Knowing where to go to replenish your soul and recharge your batteries both physically and spiritually is important and worth serious consideration. Some Capricorns may gravitate towards the mountains and many may enjoy mountain climbing or trekking, or snow sports. For others, the sea resonates for escape, but in both cases there's a tendency to enjoy activity holidays, whatever form these take.

Wherever they hail from, there are also a number of countries where Capricorn will feel comfortable, whether they choose to go there to live, work or just take a holiday. These include the UK, Bulgaria, the Sudan and Haiti, all of which resonate with grounded Capricorn energy.

When it comes to holidays, Capricorn often opts for the pleasures of a natural habitat, whether this is walking or trekking along mountain or coastal paths, or activities that include practical fun like learning to paint or cook local cuisine. City breaks also hold their appeal and in particular visits to those that have Capricorn energy, including Delhi, Chicago, Brussels, Mexico City and Oxford, UK.

CAPRI

WOMAN

CORN

Capricorn women are often distinguished by good facial bone structure, giving them a look of definition and purpose that chimes with their personality traits. They tend to move and speak in a sure-footed and decisive manner too, all of which instil their partner, family, friends and work colleagues with confidence. This is a lovely aspect of Capricorn women but it can sometimes be mistaken for a desire for independence, suggesting to others that she has no wish to be taken care of, which is not too the case. She needs love as much as the next woman and, usually, her self-awareness and ability for straight talking should help avoid her needs being ignored or taken for granted, another favourable trait.

She may not make this obvious, but for all their practical and pragmatic nature Capricorn women love to be romanced and to be reassured of their lovability. It's the one area where they are sometimes less secure than other sun signs, partly because they take nothing for granted and like to check out all the facts. But therein lies a conundrum because other people are seldom as straightforward as a fact sheet, and she will need time (remember she is ruled by Saturn) to get to know and trust someone. This can come across as unnecessarily cautious, but once she's sure of her footing in a relationship, Capricorn woman will relax, although it may take some time and reassuring behaviour on the part of any suitor.

It's important not to forget either that there's a sensuality to this sun sign, as with the other earth signs, and in combination with being a cardinal sign this means that intimacy and sex is going to be really important to this woman and feature strongly in any relationship. In fact, with some Capricorn women, given their rather reserved demeanour, this can come as something of a surprise.

Capricorn is also an extremely good listener, which is one of the ways that she gathers the facts needed to make any decision about someone. It's part of her discerning nature, although it can make her appear rather cool in attitude. She really values her friends though, and is loyal and kind in return, just as long as they don't let her down. Friendships are often for life as there's nothing fickle in her approach to these, and those who are her friends value this highly too.

CAPRI

M A
N

CORN

Often very masculine in appearance, Capricorn men have a strength of character that isn't just physical but comes from their focused energy and practical approach to life. Even if they are dressed in a classy suit and tie, they are often exactly the man you need when there's a tyre to be changed on the car, or a set of shelves to be built (although their female counterparts are often just as proficient). And if they don't know how to do something immediately, they are happy to take the time to work out how, and get it done properly once and for all.

Mr Reliable, Competent or Proficient may not be how they *wish* to be known, because they too have a romantic streak, but it's often how they show up. There's no fuss, because making a fuss wastes time, but don't underestimate their more creative side, which, combined with this practical streak, often means they are streets ahead of any competitor, whatever the stakes. Being a grounded action man is not the sum total however, because in spite of strong self-discipline, Capricorn also has a light-hearted, fun side and a great sense of humour, and he loves to relax, socialise and party well, once the work is done.

They also have a strongly creative side, which often comes through in their work, but also in romantic relationships, and creating a family life with children is often very important to them. At first glance Capricorn men may not be obvious risk-takers when it comes to love, but they know their own value and pitch high, delivering in unexpected ways given their rather pragmatic attitude in other areas, because love is very important to this man. This side of their personality is often Capricorn's best-kept secret, and those in the know often guard it well because they make extremely loyal lovers and partners. That said, they take time to form relationships and seldom make a move until they are sure about the next step. But, once decided, their focus will take a lot to shift because they don't commit lightly.

CAPRICORN
IN LOVE

Ruled by Saturn, many Capricorns can find approaching love a little difficult because life is often a rather serious business and they find the fun, flirtatious side of romance doesn't always come easily. Ideally, Capricorn would like to issue a questionnaire and base their love life on its answers, but unfortunately love's not as logical as that and they need to resist Saturn's urge to make it so. Luckily, harnessing their creative, action-oriented side works to their advantage and can help counteract this, and once Capricorn has found a suitable subject for their attention, they will make the moves necessary to court them. Sometimes this can take the recipient of their attention by surprise as they may not have realised that an invitation for an after-work drink was actually a date. But this is often how Capricorn will work at first, refusing to raise expectations and taking their time to be sure of their own romantic feelings.

CAPRICORN
AS A LOVER

Contrary to all that expected Saturn self-discipline, Capricorn in love can be one of the more romantic of the sun signs, going to a lot of time and trouble to set the scene for any seduction. But they will usually take their time, from foreplay to climax! As with the other earth signs, Capricorn's sex drive is usually strong and a desire to meet their equal is a motivating factor in their choice of lover. There's an interesting mix of caution and bravado when they make their first move, but this is a sign that often improves sexually with age, thanks to Saturn's powerful influence on time.

Self-discipline and control in the bedroom means Capricorn is usually concerned with the pleasure of their partner. Although they value their own sexual fulfilment, this sign is also conscious that equality in one another's pleasure makes things even more erotically satisfying. And although they are capable of spontaneity, Capricorn is more usually turned on by the 'deep, deep peace of the double bed' rather than 'the hurly-burly of the *chaise longue*' because, at heart, they need to feel secure in order to fully express themselves.

Capricorn is also a sign with a strong need for intellectual stimulation, because they like to talk and listen and enjoy sharing thoughts, ideas and dreams with another – and that is part of what they find sexually attractive. For Capricorn the physical side usually needs to be rooted in a strong mental connection in order to endure.

Sexual fidelity is usually important to Capricorn too, for a number of reasons. They don't give their hearts easily and seldom want to waste time playing the field when they could be spending time investing in a loving, intimate relationship that bears fruit.

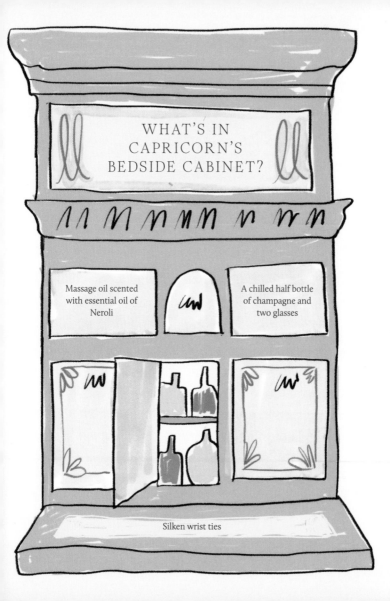

WHICH
SIGN SUITS
CAPRICORN?

In relationships with Capricorn, the sun sign of the other person and the ruling planet of that sign can bring out the best, or sometimes the worst, in a lover. Knowing what might spark, smoulder or suffocate love is worth closer investigation, but always remember that sun sign astrology is only a starting point for any relationship.

CAPRICORN
AND ARIES

Saturn and Mars can be a good love match and they are both cardinal, action-oriented signs which creates a strong emotional and physical bond, just as long as one doesn't try to overpower the other.

CAPRICORN
AND TAURUS

Two earth signs, Taurus' Venus is very attractive to Saturn, who finds their love can temper some of that Saturn discipline. Although issues around fidelity are less of a problem, there can be moments of jealousy on both sides.

CAPRICORN
AND GEMINI

Gemini's airy, fun-loving nature is often very attractive to the more controlled side of Capricorn, which in turn can help ground Mercury's capriciousness, but there may always be a bit of tension between these two aspects of character.

CAPRICORN
AND CANCER

Opposite signs often do attract, and Cancer's need for security plays well to Capricorn's need for the same, and even though Saturn can be a powerfully dominant energy, the Moon can balance this with its own gentle power.

CAPRICORN
AND LEO

Leo's ruling Sun rules the house of creativity and is any match for Saturn's powerful aspirations, but all that exuberance and ego has a tendency to make Capricorn feel a little insecure unless they can use that fiery energy to their advantage.

CAPRICORN
AND VIRGO

Two earth signs that understand the need for boundaries, although this is tempered by Virgo's mercurial aspect which can intrigue Capricorn, sparking an attraction that will probably rely on their similarities to secure the relationship.

CAPRICORN AND LIBRA

Venus exerts a big attraction for Capricorn, gifting Libra with charm and charisma, but even though they are both cardinal, action-oriented signs, Libra's airiness may prove just too fickle and insecure for this to last.

CAPRICORN AND SCORPIO

Like Capricorn, Scorpio has issues around insecurity in relationships and the sign's deep Pluto aspects finds Saturn reassuring while also being able to appreciate Capricorn's need to feel secure, which can make this an unexpectedly good match.

CAPRICORN AND SAGITTARIUS

Bounteous Jupiter instils Sagittarius with the sort of adventurous desire to journey that appeals to Capricorn, and although they may differ about how to go about it, if they can agree, then Saturn's energy is truly fired up by this fire sign.

CAPRICORN
AND CAPRICORN

They understand each and particularly their need to feel secure, but their powerful Saturn energy may play out in different ways, and they may inadvertently restrict and hinder each other's dreams. But, if not, this can be a very harmonious union.

CAPRICORN
AND AQUARIUS

Powerful Uranus can make Aquarius a little too unpredictable for those whose Saturn influence makes them rather staid, although the lighter touch of the air sign can work very well with Capricorn's creativity, and together they can change their world.

CAPRICORN
AND PISCES

Dreamy Pisces, ruled by the planet Neptune, can help Capricorn tune in to their inner ideas and aspirations, while this action-oriented sign does much to help a water sign stay on track and deliver on theirs, making this a well-balanced match.

CAPRICORN
AT WORK

areer success is virtually guaranteed with this sign and this also means Capricorn is often very financially successful too. When it comes to entrepreneurial success, for example, Capricorn's sense of timing is often excellent because they excel at discerning when to make their move, knowing when to speculate on a situation or when to pause. Although Capricorn can appear very lucky, they don't rely on luck; it's down to astute observation of market trends and this is where their creativity, combined with diligence, scores so well.

However, financial success is less of a motivator than a by-product. Capricorn's main aim is to enjoy what they have to spend time doing and because they usually enjoy the process of work, this often means they take their time to find out what they really want to do. Their grounded, personable nature often makes them good team players, but it's their commitment to the slog and to the end result that can make them strong leaders. Industries that combine creativity with practical know-how tend to attract Capricorns, whether that's architecture, theatrical production or engineering – you'll often find someone who's Capricorn, or has strong Capricorn influence in the birth chart, at the helm. The law in one form or another can also attract those Capricorns who like listening to and processing evidence and information.

Often Capricorn moves through a variety of careers but if you look at the trajectory of their professional life, it's often clear that they were learning something useful at each stage that they could transfer into the next, sowing the seeds for the next stage. Sometimes this is conscious but often it comes naturally to Capricorn. They just take the practical steps necessary in order to progress their career, knowing that, in time, it will pay off. They are usually right, and happy to build on their expertise and experience. For example, doing a postgraduate accountancy qualification which they can then utilise later as the CFO of their own creative business.

CAPRICORN
AT HOME

O ften very well organised and practical, Capricorn usually expresses this in their home too. They like order and to create an attractive home that works, with facilities that save time. Capricorn also expects things to last, so will often invest in a really good customised kitchen made of sustainable materials. Although they may have to wait a few years in order to be able to afford the home they really want to create for themselves, they are likely to show evidence of this inclination for durability even in a rental apartment. This is not someone for whom throwaway plastic is attractive.

It's not immediately apparent that family life is likely to be important to Capricorn, but this is another area in which they like to create and invest for the future. So at an early stage of home-owning, occupying or creating, Capricorn may already be factoring in space for potential offspring, or working out how they can get a return on one property investment that will help them realise another for this purpose. They are pragmatic about how long it may take and content to work towards this, putting one foot in front of the other to achieve it.

Like other earth signs, an outdoor space where they can create a garden to enjoy is often important, whether this is a balcony, sunny courtyard or several acres of green. Capricorn doesn't mind that it takes time for plants to grow, whether this is culinary herbs planted from seed, a copse of silver birch trees or containers full of spring bulbs. Saturn likes to invest in future growth and where better than in the natural world, also ruled by Pan, the original source of Capricorn's energy?

FREE THE
SPIRIT

Understanding your own sun sign astrology is only part of the picture. It provides you with a template to examine and reflect on your own life's journey but also the context for this through your relationships with others, intimate or otherwise, and within the culture and environment in which you live.

Throughout time, the Sun and planets of our universe have kept to their paths and astrologers have used this ancient wisdom to understand the pattern of the universe. In this way, astrology is a tool to utilise these wisdoms, a way of helping make sense of the energies we experience as the planets shift in our skies.

'A physician without a knowledge of astrology has no right to call himself a physician,' said Hippocrates, the Greek physician born in 460 BC, who understood better than anyone how these psychic energies worked. As did Carl Jung, the 20th-century philosopher and psychoanalyst, because he said, 'Astrology represents the summation of all the psychological knowledge of antiquity.'

THE 10
PLANETS

SUN

RULES THE ASTROLOGICAL SIGN OF LEO

Although the Sun is officially a star, for the purpose
of astrology it's considered a planet. It is also the
centre of our universe and gives us both light and
energy; our lives are dependent on it and it embodies
our creative life force. As a life giver, the Sun is
considered a masculine entity, the patriarch and
ruler of the skies. Our sun sign is where we start our
astrological journey whichever sign it falls in, and as
long as we know which day of which month we were
born, we have this primary knowledge.

MOON

RULES THE ASTROLOGICAL SIGN OF CANCER

We now know that the Moon is actually a natural satellite of the Earth (the third planet from the sun) rather than a planet but is considered such for the purposes of astrology. It's dependent on the Sun for its reflected light, and it is only through their celestial relationship that we can see it. In this way, the Moon in each of our birth charts depicts the feminine energy to balance the masculine sun's life force, the ying to its yang. It is not an impotent or subservient presence, particularly when you consider how it gives the world's oceans their tides, the relentless energy of the ebb and flow powering up the seas. The Moon's energy also helps illuminate our unconscious desires, helping to bring these to the service of our self-knowledge.

MERCURY

RULES THE ASTROLOGICAL SIGNS OF GEMINI AND VIRGO

Mercury, messenger of the gods, has always been associated with speed and agility, whether in body or mind. Because of this, Mercury is considered to be the planet of quick wit and anything requiring verbal dexterity and the application of intelligence. Those with Mercury prominent in their chart love exchanging and debating ideas and telling stories (often with a tendency to embellish the truth of a situation), making them prominent in professions where these qualities are valuable.

Astronomically, Mercury is the closest planet to the sun and moves around a lot in our skies. What's also relevant is that several times a year Mercury appears to be retrograde (see page 99) which has the effect of slowing down or disrupting its influence.

VENUS

RULES THE ASTROLOGICAL SIGNS OF TAURUS AND LIBRA

The goddess of beauty, love and pleasure. Venus is the second planet from the sun and benefits from this proximity, having received its positive vibes. Depending on which astrological sign Venus falls in your chart will influence how you relate to art and culture and the opposite sex. The characteristics of this sign will tell you all you need to know about what you aspire to, where you seek and how you experience pleasure, along with the types of lover you attract. Again, partly depending on where it's placed, Venus can sometimes increase self-indulgence which can be a less positive aspect of a hedonistic life.

MARS

RULES THE ASTROLOGICAL SIGN OF ARIES

This big, powerful planet is fourth from the sun and exerts an energetic force, powering up the characteristics of the astrological sign in which it falls in your chart. This will tell you how you assert yourself, whether your anger flares or smoulders, what might stir your passion and how you express your sexual desires. Mars will show you what works best for you to turn ideas into action, the sort of energy you might need to see something through and how your independent spirit can be most effectively engaged.

JUPITER

Big, bountiful Jupiter is the largest planet in our solar
system and fifth from the sun. It heralds optimism,
generosity and general benevolence. Whichever sign
Jupiter falls in in your chart is where you will find
the characteristics for your particular experience of
luck, happiness and good fortune. Jupiter will show
you which areas to focus on to gain the most and
best from your life. Wherever Jupiter appears in your
chart it will bring a positive influence and when it's
prominent in our skies we all benefit.

SATURN

Saturn is considered akin to Old Father Time, with all the patience, realism and wisdom that archetype evokes. Sometimes called the taskmaster of the skies, its influence is all about how we handle responsibility and it requires that we graft and apply ourselves in order to learn life's lessons. The sixth planet from the sun, Saturn's 'return' (see page 100) to its place in an individual's birth chart occurs approximately every 28 years. How self-disciplined you are about overcoming opposition or adversity will be influenced by the characteristics of the sign in which this powerful planet falls in your chart.

URANUS

RULES THE ASTROLOGICAL SIGN OF AQUARIUS

The seventh planet from the sun, Uranus is the planet of unpredictability, change and surprise, and whether you love or loathe the impact of Uranus will depend in part on which astrological sign it influences in your chart. How you respond to its influence is entirely up to the characteristics of the sign it occupies in your chart. Whether you see the change it heralds as a gift or a curse is up to you, but because it takes seven years to travel through a sign, its presence in a sign can influence a generation.

NEPTUNE

Neptune ruled the sea, and this planet is all about deep waters of mystery, imagination and secrets. It's also representative of our spiritual side so the characteristics of whichever astrological sign it occupies in your chart will influence how this plays out in your life. Neptune is the eighth planet from the sun and its influence can be subtle and mysterious. The astrological sign in which it falls in your chart will indicate how you realise your vision, dream and goals. The only precaution is if it falls in an equally watery sign, creating a potential difficulty in distinguishing between fantasy and reality.

PLUTO

Pluto is the furthest planet from the sun and exerts
a regenerative energy that transforms but often
requires destruction to erase what's come before in
order to begin again. Its energy often lies dormant
and then erupts, so the astrological sign in which it
falls will have a bearing on how this might play out in
your chart. Transformation can be very positive but
also very painful. When Pluto's influence is strong,
change occurs and how you react or respond to this
will be very individual. Don't fear it, but reflect on
how to use its energy to your benefit.

♑   CAPRICORN

YOUR SUN SIGN

Your sun or zodiac sign is the one in which you were born, determined by the date of your birth. Your sun sign is ruled by a specific planet. For example, Capricorn is ruled by Saturn but Gemini by Mercury, so we already have the first piece of information and the first piece of our individual jigsaw puzzle.

The next piece of the jigsaw is understanding that the energy of a particular planet in your birth chart (see page 78) plays out via the characteristics of the astrological sign in which it's positioned, and this is hugely valuable in understanding some of the patterns of your life. You may have your Sun in Capricorn, and a good insight into the characteristics of this sign, but what if you have Neptune in Leo? Or Venus in Aries? Uranus in Virgo? Understanding the impact of these influences can help you reflect on the way you react or respond and the choices you can make, helping to ensure more positive outcomes.

If, for example, with Uranus in Taurus you are resistant to change, remind yourself that change is inevitable and can be positive, allowing you to work with it rather than against its influence. If you have Neptune in Virgo, it will bring a more spiritual element to this practical earth sign, while Mercury in Aquarius will enhance the predictive element of your analysis and judgement. The scope and range and useful aspect of having this knowledge is just the beginning of how you can utilise astrology to live your best life.

PLANETS IN TRANSIT

In addition, the planets do not stay still. They are said to transit (move) through the course of an astrological year. Those closest to us, like Mercury, transit quite regularly (every 88 days), while those further away, like Pluto, take much longer, in this case 248 years to come full circle. So the effects of each planet can vary depending on their position and this is why we hear astrologers talk about someone's Saturn return (see page 100), Mercury retrograde (see page 99) or about Capricorn (or other sun sign) 'weather'. This is indicative of an influence that can be anticipated and worked with and is both universal and personal. The shifting positions of the planets bring an influence to bear on each of us, linked to the position of our own planetary influences and how these have a bearing on each other. If you understand the nature of these planetary influences you can begin to work with, rather than against, them and this information can be very much to your benefit. First, though, you need to take a look at the component parts of astrology, the pieces of your personal jigsaw, then you'll have the information you need to make sense of how your sun sign might be affected during the changing patterns of the planets.

YOUR BIRTH CHART

With the date, time and place of birth, you can easily find out where your (or anyone else's) planets are positioned from an online astrological chart programme (see page 110). This will give you an exact sun sign position, which you probably already know, but it can also be useful if you think you were born 'on the cusp' because it will give you an *exact* indication of what sign you were born in. In addition, this natal chart will tell you your Ascendant sign, which sign your Moon is in, along with the other planets specific to your personal and completely individual chart and the Houses (see page 81) in which the astrological signs are positioned.

A birth chart is divided into 12 sections, representing each of the 12 Houses (see pages 82–85) with your Ascendant or Rising sign always positioned in the 1st House, and the other 11 Houses running counter-clockwise from 1 to 12.

ASCENDANT OR RISING SIGN

Your Ascendant is a first, important part of the complexity of an individual birth chart. While your sun sign gives you an indication of the personality you will inhabit through the course of your life, it is your Ascendant or Rising sign – which is the sign rising at the break of dawn on the Eastern horizon at the time and on the date of your birth – that often gives a truer indication of how you will project your personality and consequently how the world sees you. So even though you were born a sun sign Taurus, whatever sign your Ascendant is in, for example Cancer, will be read through the characteristics of this astrological sign.

Your Ascendant is always in your 1st House, which is the House of the Self (see page 82) and the other houses always follow the same consecutive astrological order. So if, for example, your Ascendant is Leo, then your second house is in Virgo, your third house in Libra, and so on. Each House has its own characteristics but how these will play out in your individual chart will be influenced by the sign positioned in it.

Opposite your Ascendant is your Descendant sign, positioned in the 7th House (see page 84) and this shows what you look for in a partnership, your complementary 'other half' as it were. There's always something intriguing about what the Descendant can help us to understand, and it's worth knowing yours and being on the lookout for it when considering a long-term marital or business partnership.

THE 12 HOUSES

While each of the 12 Houses represent different aspects of our lives, they are also ruled by one of the 12 astrological signs, giving each house its specific characteristics. When we discover, for example, that we have Capricorn in the 12th House, this might suggest a pragmatic or practical approach to spirituality. Or, if you had Gemini in your 6th House, this might suggest a rather airy approach to organisation.

1ST HOUSE

RULED BY ARIES

The first impression you give walking into a room, how you like to be seen, your sense of self and the energy with which you approach life.

2ND HOUSE

RULED BY TAURUS

What you value, including what you own that provides your material security; your self-value and work ethic, how you earn your income.

3RD HOUSE

RULED BY GEMINI

How you communicate through words, deeds and gestures; also how you learn and function in a group, including within your own family.

4 TH HOUSE

RULED BY CANCER

This is about your home, your security
and how you take care of yourself and
your family; and also about those family
traditions you hold dear.

5 TH HOUSE

RULED BY LEO

Creativity in all its forms, including fun
and eroticism, intimate relationships and
procreation, self-expression
and positive fulfilment.

6 TH HOUSE

RULED BY VIRGO

How you organise your daily routine, your
health, your business affairs, and how you
are of service to others, from those
in your family to the workplace.

7TH HOUSE

RULED BY LIBRA

This is about partnerships and shared
goals, whether marital or in business,
and what we look for in these to
complement ourselves.

8TH HOUSE

RULED BY SCORPIO

Regeneration, through death and rebirth,
and also our legacy and how this might be
realised through sex, procreation
and progeny.

9TH HOUSE

RULED BY SAGITTARIUS

Our world view, cultures outside our
own and the bigger picture beyond our
immediate horizon, to which we travel
either in body or mind.

10TH HOUSE

RULED BY CAPRICORN

Our aims and ambitions in life, what we aspire
to and what we're prepared to do to achieve it;
this is how we approach our
working lives.

11TH HOUSE

RULED BY AQUARIUS

The house of humanity and our
friendships, our relationships with the
wider world, our tribe or group to which
we feel an affiliation.

12TH HOUSE

RULED BY PISCES

Our spiritual side resides here. Whether this
is religious or not, it embodies our inner life,
beliefs and the deeper connections we forge.

THE FOUR
ELEMENTS

The 12 astrological signs are divided into four groups,
representing the four elements: fire, water, earth and air.
This gives each of the three signs in each group additional
characteristics.

FIRE

ARIES ~ LEO ~ SAGITTARIUS

Embodying warmth, spontaneity and enthusiasm.

WATER

CANCER ~ SCORPIO ~ PISCES

Embody a more feeling, spiritual and intuitive side.

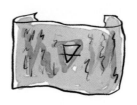

EARTH

TAURUS ☙ VIRGO ☙ CAPRICORN

Grounded and sure-footed and sometimes rather stubborn.

AIR

GEMINI ❧ LIBRA ❧ AQUARIUS

Flourishing in the world of vision, ideas and perception.

FIXED, CARDINAL OR MUTABLE?

The 12 signs are further divided into three groups of four, giving additional characteristics of being fixed, cardinal or mutable. These represent the way in which they respond to situations.

FIXED

TAURUS, LEO, SCORPIO AND AQUARIUS
ARE FIXED SIGNS

Their energy tends to be steady and they are less
reactive, more responsive, although they can have
a tendency to be resistant to change and need
encouragement.

CARDINAL

ARIES, CANCER, LIBRA AND
CAPRICORN ARE CARDINAL SIGNS

Their energy is often instinctive and action-oriented,
enabling them to get things started, although there's
sometimes a tendency to fail to carry things through.

MUTABLE

GEMINI, VIRGO, SAGITTARIUS AND
PISCES ARE MUTABLE SIGNS

The clue here is their adaptability and responsiveness to
change, which they don't fear, and readiness to listen to
and embrace new ideas.

MERCURY RETROGRADE

This occurs several times over the astrological year and lasts for around four weeks, with a shadow week either side (a quick Google search will tell you the forthcoming dates). It's important what sign Mercury is in while it's retrograde, because its impact will be affected by the characteristics of that sign. For example, if Mercury is retrograde in Gemini, the sign of communication that is ruled by Mercury, the effect will be keenly felt in all areas of communication. However, if Mercury is retrograde in Aquarius, which rules the house of friendships and relationships, this may keenly affect our communication with large groups, or if in Sagittarius, which rules the house of travel, it could affect travel itineraries and encourage us to check our documents carefully.

Mercury retrograde can also be seen as an opportunity to pause, review or reconsider ideas and plans, to regroup, recalibrate and recuperate, and generally to take stock of where we are and how we might proceed. In our fast-paced 24/7 lives, Mercury retrograde can often be a useful opportunity to slow down and allow ourselves space to restore some necessary equilibrium.

SATURN RETURN

When the planet Saturn returns to the place in your chart that it occupied at the time of your birth, it has an impact. This occurs roughly every 28 years, so we can see immediately that it correlates with ages that we consider representative of different life stages and when we might anticipate change or adjustment to a different era. At 28 we can be considered at full adult maturity, probably established in our careers and relationships, maybe with children; at 56 we have reached middle age and are possibly at another of life's crossroads; and at 84, we might be considered at the full height of our wisdom, our lives almost complete. If you know the time and place of your birth date, an online Saturn return calculator can give you the exact timing.

It will also be useful to identify in which astrological sign Saturn falls in your chart, which will help you reflect on its influence, as both influences can be very illuminating about how you will experience and manage the impact of its return. Often the time leading up to a personal Saturn return is a demanding one, but the lessons learnt help inform the decisions made about how to progress your own goals. Don't fear this period, but work with its influence: knowledge is power and Saturn has a powerful energy you can harness should you choose.

THE MINOR PLANETS

Sun sign astrology seldom makes mention of these 'minor' planets that also orbit the sun, but increasingly their subtle influence is being referenced. If you have had your birth chart done (if you know your birth time and place you can do this online) you will have access to this additional information.

Like the 10 main planets on the previous pages, these 18 minor entities will also be positioned in an astrological sign, bringing their energy to bear on these characteristics. You may, for example, have Fortuna in Leo, or Diana in Sagittarius. Look to these for their subtle influences on your birth chart and life via the sign they inhabit, all of which will serve to animate and resonate further the information you can reference on your own personal journey.

AESCULAPIA

Jupiter's grandson and a powerful healer, Aesculapia was taught by Chiron and influences us in what could be life-saving action, realised through the characteristics of the sign in which it falls in our chart.

BACCHUS

Jupiter's son, Bacchus is similarly benevolent but can sometimes lack restraint in the pursuit of pleasure. How this plays out in your chart is dependent on the sign in which it falls.

APOLLO

Jupiter's son, gifted in art, music and healing, Apollo rides the Sun across the skies. His energy literally lights up the way in which you inspire others, characterised by the sign in which it falls in your chart.

CERES

Goddess of agriculture and mother of Proserpina, Ceres is associated with the seasons and how we manage cycles of change in our lives. This energy is influenced by the sign in which it falls in our chart.

CHIRON

Teacher of the gods, Chiron knew all about healing herbs and medical practices and he lends his energy to how we tackle the impossible or the unthinkable, that which seems difficult to do.

DIANA

Jupiter's independent daughter was allowed to run free without the shackles of marriage. Where this falls in your birth chart will indicate what you are not prepared to sacrifice in order to conform.

CUPID

Son of Venus. The sign into which Cupid falls will influence how you inspire love and desire in others, not always appropriately and sometimes illogically but it can still be an enduring passion.

FORTUNA

Jupiter's daughter, who is always shown blindfolded, influences your fated role in other people's lives, how you show up for them without really understanding why, and at the right time.

HYGEIA

Daughter of Aesculapia and also associated with health, Hygeia is about how you anticipate risk and the avoidance of unwanted outcomes. The way you do this is characterised by the sign in which Hygeia falls.

MINERVA

Another of Jupiter's daughters, depicted by an owl, will show you via the energy given to a particular astrological sign in your chart how you show up at your most intelligent and smart. How you operate intellectually.

JUNO

Juno was the wife of Jupiter and her position in your chart will indicate where you will make a commitment in order to feel safe and secure. It's where you might seek protection in order to flourish.

OPS

The wife of Saturn, Ops saved the life of her son Jupiter by giving her husband a stone to eat instead of him. Her energy in our chart enables us to find positive solutions to life's demands and dilemmas.

PANACEA

Gifted with healing powers, Panacea
provides us with a remedy for all ills
and difficulties, and how this plays
out in your life will depend on the
characteristics of the astrological sign
in which her energy falls.

PSYCHE

Psyche, Venus' daughter-in-law, shows
us that part of ourselves that is easy to
love and endures through adversity,
and your soul that survives death and
flies free, like the butterfly that
depicts her.

PROSERPINA

Daughter of Ceres, abducted by Pluto,
Proserpina has to spend her life divided
between earth and the underworld and
she represents how we bridge the gulf
between different and difficult aspects
of our lives.

SALACIA

Neptune's wife, Salacia stands on
the seashore bridging land and sea,
happily bridging the two realities.
In your chart, she shows how you
can harmoniously bring two sides of
yourself together.

VESTA

Daughter of Saturn, Vesta's job was to protect Rome and in turn she was protected by vestal virgins. Her energy influences how we manage our relationships with competitive females and male authority figures.

VULCAN

Vulcan was a blacksmith who knew how to control fire and fashion metal into shape, and through the sign in which it falls in your chart will show you how you control your passion and make it work for you.

FURTHER READING

Jung's Studies in Astrology: Prophecies, Magic and the Qualities of Time,

Liz Greene, Routledge (2018)

Lunar Oracle: Harness the Power of the Moon,

Liberty Phi, OH Editions (2021)

Metaphysics of Astrology: Why Astrology Works,

Ivan Antic, Independently published (2020)

*Parkers' Astrology: The Definitive Guide to Using Astrology in Every Aspect
of Your Life*,

Julia and Derek Parker, Dorling Kindersley (2020)

USEFUL WEBSITES

Alicebellastrology.com
Astro.com
Astrology.com
Cafeastrology.com
Costarastrology.com
Jessicaadams.com

USEFUL APPS

Astro Future
Co-Star
Moon
Sanctuary
Time Nomad
Time Passages

ACKNOWLEDGEMENTS

Thanks are due to my Taurean publisher Kate Pollard for commissioning this Astrology Oracle series, to Piscean Matt Tomlinson for his careful editing, and to Evi O Studio for their beautiful design and illustrations.

ABOUT THE AUTHOR

As a sun sign Aquarius Liberty Phi loves to explore the world and has lived on three different continents, currently residing in North America. Their Gemini moon inspires them to communicate their love of astrology and other esoteric practices while Leo rising helps energise them. Their first publication, also released by OH Editions, is a box set of 36 oracle cards and accompanying guide, entitled *Lunar Oracle: Harness the Power of the Moon*.

Published in 2023 by OH Editions,
an imprint of Welbeck Non-Fiction Ltd,
part of the Welbeck Publishing Group.
Offices in London, 20 Mortimer Street, London, W1T 3JW,
and Sydney, 205 Commonwealth Street, Surry Hills, 2010.
www.welbeckpublishing.com

Design © 2023 OH Editions
Text © 2023 Liberty Phi
Illustrations © 2023 Evi O. Studio

A CIP catalogue record for this book is available from the British Library.

ISBN 978-1-80453-002-3

Publisher: Kate Pollard
Editor: Sophie Elletson
In-house editor: Matt Tomlinson
Designer: Evi O. Studio
Illustrator: Evi O. Studio
Production controller: Jess Brisley
Printed and bound by Leo Paper

MIX
Paper | Supporting
responsible forestry
FSC® C020056
www.fsc.org

10 9 8 7 6 5 4 3 2 1